GW01044298

RECIPE FOR A HAPPY LIFE

WRITTEN BY
MARGARET OF NAVARRE

IN THE YEAR FIFTEEN HUNDRED

Amplified by a Compilation from the Works of Various Writers byMarie West King

NEW YORK

Recipe for a Happy Life

 For information, address Cosimo, P.O. Box 416, Old Chelsea Station, New York, NY 10113-0416, or visit our website at www.cosimobooks.com.

Recipe for a Happy Life was originally published by Paul Elder and Company in 1911.

Library of Congress Cataloging-in-Publication Data
A catalog record for this book is available from the Library of Congress

Cover design by smythtype

ISBN: 1-59605-040-3

Margaret of Angoulême, Queen of Navarre and chief patroness of letters in the early half of the sixteenth century, was also a poet and writer herself of no mean degree. A woman of broad religious interests, serious and learned for her time, a time when women were seldom either serious or learned, she has combined for us today, as well as for her own generation, the sane ingredients for a well rounded and happy life. It is a long way back to her day and in many details of morals and of manners life has assumed changed aspects, but we feel anew, when we read her words, that it is forever unchangeable in its essentials.

Marie West King has thoughtfully selected passages from later writers, expanding the suggestions in Queen Margaret's "Recipe for a Happy Life," and opening for us many pleasant by-paths for their application.

The thoughts so delightfully chosen by Miss King are culled from the literature of the ages, and there are bits from younger and some from much older writers than Margaret of Navarre. Many are of that quality which does not die; others are merely appealing little sayings which, being colloquially stated, pass away with their generation, but their essence being permanent they are constantly being resurrected in new form, as blossoms which bloom and fade and bloom again.

Surely, no beautiful thing can die.

Recipe for a Happy Life

Written by Margaret of Navarre in the Year Fifteen Hundred

THREE ounces are necessary, first of [2]*Patience*,
Then, of [8]*Repose & Peace;* of [14]*Conscience*
A pound entire is needful;
Of [20]*Pastimes* of all sorts, too,
Should be gathered as much as the hand can hold;
Of [26]*Pleasant Memory* & of *Hope* three good drachms
There must be at least. But they should moistened be
With a liquor made from [33]*True Pleasures* which rejoice the heart.
Then of [37]*Love's Magic Drops*, a few—
But use them sparingly, for they may bring a flame
Which naught but tears can drown.
Grind the whole and mix therewith of [44]*Merriment*, an ounce
To even. Yet all this may not bring happiness
Except in your [50]*Orisons* you lift your voice
To Him who holds the gift of health.

NOTE: The text following is subdivided under the heads of the "ingredients" of the Recipe, the numerals 2, 8, 14, 20, 26, 33, 37, 44 and 50 referring to the commencing pages.

Patience

However sore to flesh and blood,
I hold this thing as true;
The way that God selects,—appoints
Is ever best for you.

However sharp the flints that press
The tender feet, unshod;
I hold the roughest path may lead
To closer walk with God.

—Mrs. Mary M. Gunnison.

Patience is a plant
That grows not in all gardens.

—Longfellow.

Come what come may,
Time and the hour runs through the roughest day.

—Shakespeare.

Patience is powerful.

—Longfellow.

Patience

Patience; accomplish thy labor; accomplish thy work of affection!
Sorrow and silence are strong, and patient endurance is godlike.
Therefore accomplish thy labor of love, till the heart is made godlike,
Purified, strengthened, perfected, and rendered more worthy of heaven.

—Longfellow.

There is a day of sunny rest
For every dark and troubled night;
And grief may bide an evening guest,
But joy shall come with early light.

* * * * *

For God hath marked each sorrowing day
And numbered every secret tear,
And heaven's long age of bliss shall pay
For all his children suffer here.

—Bryant.

One day at a time.

—Selected.

Patience

Be still, sad heart, and cease repining;
Behind the clouds is the sun still shining;
Thy fate is the common fate of all,
Into each life some rain must fall,
Some days must be dark and dreary.

—LONGFELLOW.

Let nothing disturb thee,
Nothing affright thee;
All things are passing;
God never changeth;
Patient endurance
Attaineth to all things;
Who God possesseth
In nothing is wanting,
Alone God sufficeth.

—LONGFELLOW.

Endurance is the crowning quality,
And patience all the passion of great hearts.

—LOWELL.

Self conquest is the greatest of victories.

—PLATO.

Patience

Joggin' Erlong

De da'kest hour, dey allus say,
Is des' befo' de dawn,
But it's moughty ha'd a-waitin'
W'ere de night goes frownin' on;
An' it's moughty ha'd a-hopin'
W'en de clouds is big an' black,
An' all de t'ings you's waited for
Has failed, er gone to wrack—
But des' keep on a-joggin' wid a little bit o' song,
De mo'n is allus brightah w'en de night's been long.

Dey's lots o' knocks you's got to tek
Befo' yo' journey's done,
An' dey's times w'en you'll be wishin'
Dat de weary race was run;
W'en you want to give up tryin'
And des' float erpon de wave,
W'en you don't feel no mo' sorrer
Ez yo' t'ink erbout de grave—
Den, des' keep on a-joggin' wid a little bit o' song,
De mo'n is allus brightah w'en de night's been long.

— Paul Laurence Dunbar.

Patience

Oft the cloud which wraps the present hour
Serves but to brighten all our future days.
— John Brown.

The Road 'll Turn Some Day

I know the road is rocky,
And the hills are hard to climb;
I know the feet get bruised and sore,
And it takes heaps o' time.
I know the burden 's heavy —
O, you need n't tempt to say;
But just keep plodding onward —
For the road 'll turn some day!

I know that homesick feeling,
And the ache you bear alone;
I know your heart is breaking,
By the bravely stifled moan.
I know the arm you leaned upon
Has now no power to stay;
But just keep a plodding onward —
For the road 'll turn some day!

Patience

I know the structures you have hewn
Of youth day-dreams lie low;
I know you see their ruins stare
Everywhere you go.
I know the sunbeams round your path
Long since have ceased to play;
But just keep a-ploddin' onward —
For the road 'll turn some day.

—SELECTED.

So nigh is grandeur to our dust,
So near is God to man;
When duty whispers low, "Thou must!"
The heart replies, "I can!"

—EMERSON.

How smooth the sea-beach pebbles are!
But, do you know?
The ocean worked a hundred years
To make them so!

—HENRIETTA R. ELIOT.

There is no crown in the world so good as patience.

—SELECTED.

Repose and Peace

THESE should be hours for necessities,
Not for delights; times to repair our nature
With comforting repose, and not for us
To waste these times.
—SHAKESPEARE.

Rest that strengthens unto virtuous deeds,
Is one with prayer.
—BAYARD TAYLOR.

There is rest for all things. On still nights
There is a folding of a million wings—
The swarming honey-bees in unknown woods,
The speckled butterflies and downy broods
In dizzy poplar heights:
Rest for innumerable nameless things,
Rest for the creatures underneath the Sea,
And in the Earth, and in the starry Air.
—T. B. ALDRICH.

In peace, there 's nothing so becomes a man
As modest stillness and humility.
—SHAKESPEARE.

Repose and Peace

Of all our loving Father's gifts,
I often wonder which is best,—
And cry: Dear God, the one that lifts
Our souls from weariness to rest,
The rest of Silence,—that is best.

—MARY CLEMMER.

Calm and unruffled as a summer sea,
When not a breath of wind flies o'er its surface.

—ADDISON.

At peace with God and the world.

—LONGFELLOW.

A gentleman makes no noise; a lady is serene.

—EMERSON.

Wise men read very sharply all your private history in your look, and gait, and behavior.

—EMERSON.

Repose and Peace

Hard work is good an' wholesome, past
all doubt;
But 'tain't so, ef the mind gits tuckered
out.
—LOWELL.

To sit as idle as the grass
Watching the clouds make pictures in the air.
—ALICE CARY.

Worry is the rust of the soul.
—SELECTED.

Silken rest
Tie all thy cares up.
—BEAUMONT & FLETCHER.

Today let us enjoy ourselves. Sorrows, joys, tears, smiles, go in and out before us. Happy the man who contentedly resigns himself to his fate.
—SELECTED.

Repose and Peace

What, what is virtue, but repose of mind,
A pure ethereal calm, that knows no storm;
Above the reach of wild Ambition's wind,
Above those passions that this world deform,
And torture man.

—THOMSON.

There was a soft and pensive grace,
A cast of thought upon her face,
That suited well the forehead high,
The eyelash dark, and downcast eye:
The mild expression spoke a mind
In duty firm, composed, resigned.

—SCOTT.

Whate'er he did was done with so much ease,
In him alone 't was natural to please.

—DRYDEN.

Soft words, with nothing in them, make a song.

—WALLER.

Repose and Peace

Peace

With eager heart and will on fire,
I fought to win my great desire;
"Peace shall be mine," I said; but life
Grew bitter in the weary strife.

My soul was tired, and my pride
Was wounded deep; to Heaven I cried,
"God grant me peace or I must die";
The dumb stars glittered no reply.

Broken at last, I bowed my head,
Forgetting all myself, and said,
"Whatever comes, His will be done";
And in that moment peace was won.

—Henry Van Dyke.

Peace is the evening star of the soul, as virtue is its sun; and the two are never far apart.

—Colton.

Repose and Peace

Have you known how to compose your manners? You have done a great deal more than he who has composed books. Have you known how to take repose? You have done more than he who has taken cities and empires.

— MONTAIGNE.

Peace does not dwell in outward things, but within the soul; we may preserve it in the midst of the bitterest pain, if our will remain firm and submissive. Peace in this life springs from acquiescence, not in an exemption from suffering.

— FÉNELON.

Nothing can bring you peace but yourself. Nothing can bring you peace but the triumph of principles.

— EMERSON.

Conscience

E THAT has light within his own clear breast,
May sit i' the centre, and enjoy bright day;
But he that hides a dark soul, and foul thoughts,
Benighted walks under the midday sun;
Himself is his own dungeon.

— MILTON.

Man's conscience is the oracle of God.

— BYRON.

He will easily be content and at peace, whose conscience is pure.

— THOMAS À KEMPIS.

Conscience is harder than our enemies,
Knows more, accuses with more nicety.

— GEORGE ELIOT.

A quiet conscience makes one so serene.

— BYRON.

Conscience

THE BELL OF THE ANGELS

There has come to my mind a legend,
A thing I had half forgot,
And, where I read it or dreamed it —
Ah, well! it matters not.

It is said in Heaven, at twilight,
A great bell so softly swings,
And man may listen and hearken
To the wondrous music that rings.

If he puts from his heart's inner chamber
All the passion, pain and strife,
Heartache and weary longing
That throb in the pulses of life.

If he thrust from his soul all hatred,
All thoughts of wicked things,
He can hear in the holy twilight
How the bell of the angels ring.

And I think there lies in the legend,
If we open our eyes to see,

Conscience

Somewhat of an inner meaning,
  My friend, to you and me.

Let us look in our hearts and question:
  Can purer thoughts enter in
To a soul, if it be already
  The dwelling of thoughts of sin?

So, then, let us ponder a little,
  Let us look in our hearts and see
If the twilight bell of the angels
  Could ring for us — you and me.

— SELECTED.

I feel within me
A peace above all earthly dignities,
A still and quiet conscience.

— SHAKESPEARE.

My conscience is my crown.

— R. SOUTHWELL.

Conscience

Today

So here hath been dawning another blue day;
Think, wilt thou let it slip useless way?

Out of eternity this new day is born;
Into eternity at night will return.

Behold it aforetime no eye ever did;
So soon it forever from all eyes is hid.

Here hath been dawning another blue day;
Think, wilt thou let it slip useless away?

— Thomas Carlyle.

Build today, then, strong and sure,
With a firm and ample base;
And ascending and secure
Shall tomorrow find its place.

— Longfellow.

Conscience is God's vicegerent on earth.

— Bowen.

Conscience

By thine own soul's law learn to live,
  And if men thwart thee take no heed,
And if men hate thee have no care;
  Sing thou thy song and do thy deed.
Hope thou thy hope and pray thy prayer,
  And claim no crown they will not give,
Nor bays they grudge thee for thy hair.

Keep thou thy soul-worn steadfast oath,
  And to thy heart be true thy heart;
What thy soul teaches learn to know,
  And play out thine appointed part,
And thou shalt reap as thou shalt sow,
  Nor helped nor hindered in thy growth,
To thy full stature thou shalt grow.

Fix on the future's goal thy face,
  And let thy feet be lured to stray
Nowhither, but be swift to run,
  And nowhere tarry by the way,
Until at last the end is won,
  And thou mayst look back from thy place,
And see thy long day's journey done.

— Beatty.

Conscience

Labor to keep alive in your breast that little spark of celestial fire, called Conscience.
—George Washington.

In the silent midnight watches,
List—thy bosom door!
How it knocketh, knocketh, knocketh,
Knocketh evermore!
Say not 't is thy pulses beating;
'T is thy heart of sin:
'T is thy Saviour knocks, and crieth,
Rise and let me in!
—A. C. Coxe.

Guard well thy thought; our thoughts are heard in heaven.
—Young.

Our acts our angels are, or good or ill,
Our fatal shadows that walk by us still.
—Fletcher.

'T is the mind that makes the body rich.
—Selected.

Pastimes

GATHER ye rosebuds while ye may,
Old Time is still a-flying;
And this same flower that smiles today,
Tomorrow will be dying.

— HERRICK.

The mind ought sometimes to be diverted, that it may return the better to thinking.

— PHÆDRUS.

Nothing more preserves men in their wits,
Than giving of them leave to play by fits,
In dreams to sport, and ramble with all fancies,
And waking, little less extravagances;
The rest and recreation of tired thought,
When 't is run down with care, and overwrought;
Of which whoever does not freely take
His constant share, is never broad awake.

— BUTLER.

Over the hills and far away.

— GAY.

Pastimes

O gift of God! O perfect day:
Whereon shall no man work, but play;
Whereon it is enough for me,
Not to be doing, but to be.

—LONGFELLOW.

Time for work,—yet take
Much holiday for art's and friendship's sake.

—GEORGE JAMES DE WILDE.

Go forth, under the open sky, and list
To Nature's teachings.

—BRYANT.

Nature ever yields reward
To him who seeks, and loves her best.

—BARRY CORNWALL.

Away! I will not be, today,
The only slave of toil and care.
Away from desk and dust! away!
I 'll be as idle as the air.

—BRYANT.

Pastimes

I am a great friend to public amusements, for they keep people from vice.

— Samuel Johnson.

Fill the bright goblet, spread the festive board,
Summon the gay, the noble, and the fair,
Let mirth and music sound the dirge of care.

— Scott.

The mind, relaxing into needful sport,
Should turn to writers of an abler sort,
Whose wit well managed, and whose classic style,
Give truth a lustre, and make wisdom smile.

— Cowper.

'T is liberty alone that gives the flow'r
Of fleeting life its lustre and perfume,
And we are weeds without it.

— Cowper.

'T is good to be abroad in the sun.

— Lowell.

Pastimes

The next method, therefore, that I would propose to fill up our time should be useful and innocent diversions.

— ADDISON.

The stage might be made a perpetual source of the most noble and useful entertainments were it under proper regulations.

— ADDISON.

But the mind never unbends itself so agreeably as in the conversation of a well-chosen friend.

— ADDISON.

A man that has a taste for music, painting, or architecture, is like one that has another sense, when compared with such as have no relish for those arts.

— ADDISON.

Mixing together profit and delight.

— HORACE.

Pastimes

When griping griefs the heart doth wound,
And doleful dumps the mind oppress,
*   *   *   *   *
Then music, with her silver sound,
With speedy help doth lend redress.

—SHAKESPEARE.

Dreams, books, are each a world; and books, we know,
Are a substantial world, both pure and good;
Round these, with tendrils strong as flesh and blood,
Our pastime and our happiness will grow.

—WORDSWORTH.

Sweet recreation barred, what doth ensue
But moody and dull melancholy.

—SHAKESPEARE.

A day for toil, an hour for sport.

—EMERSON.

Friends, books, a garden, and perhaps his pen.

—COWPER.

Pastimes

No entertainment is so cheap as reading, nor any pleasure so lasting.

— Lady M. W. Montague.

Reading serves for delight, for ornament, for ability.

— Bacon.

The love of reading enables a man to exchange the wearisome hours of life, which come to everyone, for hours of delight.

— Montesquieu.

How sweet the moonlight sleeps upon this bank!
Here will we sit, and let the sounds of music
Creep in our ears: soft stillness, and the night,
Become the touches of sweet harmony.

— Shakespeare.

We have had pastime here, and pleasing game.

— Shakespeare.

Pleasant Memory and Hope

Memories.

Oft I remember those whom I have known
In other days, to whom my heart was led
As by a magnet, and who are not dead,
But absent, and their memories overgrown
With other thoughts and troubles of my own,
As graves with grasses are, and at their head
The stone with moss and lichens so o'erspread,
Nothing is legible but the name alone.
And is it so with them? After long years,
Do they remember me in the same way,
And is the memory pleasant as to me?
I fear to ask; yet wherefore are my fears?
Pleasures, like flowers, may wither and decay,
And yet the root perennial may be.

—Longfellow.

I remember, I remember
How my childhood fleeted by,—
The mirth of its December,
And the warmth of its July.

—Praed.

Pleasant Memory and Hope

Oft in the stilly night,
Ere slumber's chain has bound me,
Fond memory brings the light
Of other days around me;
The smiles, the tears,
Of boyhood's years,
The words of love then spoken;
The eyes that shone
Now dimmed and gone,
The cheerful hearts now broken.

—THOMAS MOORE.

Sweet memory, wafted by thy gentle gale,
Oft up the stream of Time I turn my sail,
To view the fairy-haunts of long-lost hours,
Blest with far greener shades, far lovelier flowers.

—ROGERS.

I have a room whereinto no one enters
Save I myself alone;
There sits a blessed memory on a throne,
There my life centers.

—CHRISTINA G. ROSSETTI.

Pleasant Memory and Hope

They have not perished — no!
Kind words, remembered voices once so sweet,
Smiles, radiant long ago,
And features, the great soul's apparent seat.

— BRYANT.

'T is but a little faded flower,
But oh, how fondly dear!
'T will bring me back one golden hour,
Through many a weary year.

— ELLEN C. HOWARTH.

Ah! memories of sweet summer eves,
Of moonlit wave and willowy way,
Of stars and flowers, and dewy leaves,
And smiles and tones more dear than they!

— WHITTIER.

His years with others must the sweeter be
For those brief days he spent in loving me.

— GEORGE ELIOT.

For hope shall brighten days to come,
And memory gild the past.

— MOORE.

Pleasant Memory and Hope

The Hope Indomitable

King Hassan, well beloved, was wont to say,
When aught went wrong or any labor failed:
"Tomorrow, friends, will be another day!"
And in that faith he slept, and so prevailed.
Long live this proverb! While the world shall roll,
Tomorrows fresh shall rise from out the night
And new-baptize the indomitable soul
With courage for its never-ending fight.
No one, I say, is conquered till he yields,
And yield he need not, while, like mist from glass,
God wipes the stain of life's old battle-fields
From every morning that he brings to pass.
New day, new hope, new courage! Let this be,
O soul, thy cheerful creed. What 's yesterday,
With all its shards and wrack and grief to thee?
Forget it, then—here lies the victor's way.

—Selected.

Yet where an equal poise of hope and fear
Does arbitrate the event, my nature is
That I incline to hope rather than fear.

—Milton.

Pleasant Memory and Hope

After

After the darkness, dawning,
And stir of the rested wing;
Fresh fragrance from the meadow,
Fresh hope in everything.

After the winter, springtime,
And dreams, that, flower-like, throng;
After the tempest, silence;
After the silence, song.

After the heat of anger,
Love, that all life enwraps;
After the stress of battle,
The trumpet sounding "taps."

After regret and doubting,
A faith without alloy,
God here and over yonder,—
The end of all things—joy!

—Florence Earle Coates.

Hope springs eternal in the human breast.

—Pope.

Pleasant Memory and Hope

The Night is mother of the Day,
The Winter of the Spring,
And ever upon old decay
The greenest mosses cling.
Behind the cloud the starlight lurks,
Through showers the sunbeams fall;
For God, who loveth all his works,
Has left His hope with all!

— WHITTIER.

Hopes, what are they? — Beads of morning
Strung on slender blades of grass;
Or a spider's web adorning
In a straight and treacherous pass.

— WORDSWORTH.

Hope, like a cordial, innocent, though strong,
Man's heart at once inspirits and serenes,
Nor makes him pay his wisdom for his joys.

— YOUNG.

Our greatest good, and what we least can spare,
Is hope.

— JOHN ARMSTRONG.

Pleasant Memory and Hope

Hope, like the glimm'ring taper's light,
Adorns and cheers the way;
And still as darker grows the night,
Emits a brighter ray.

—GOLDSMITH.

Auspicious Hope! in thy sweet garden grow
Wreaths for each toil, a charm for every woe.

—CAMPBELL.

Work without hope draws nectar in a sieve,
And hope without an object cannot live.

—COLERIDGE.

Who bids me hope, and, in that charming word
Has peace and transport to my soul restor'd.

—LORD LYTTLETON.

But hope will make thee young, for Hope and Youth
Are children of one mother, even Love.

—SHELLEY.

True Pleasures

Out of the garden of playtime, out of the
bower of rest,
Fain would I follow at daytime, music that
calls to a quest.
Hark, how the galloping measure
Quickens the pulses of pleasure;
Gaily saluting the morn
With the long, clear note of the hunting-horn,
Echoing up from the valley,
Over the mountain side,—
Rally, you hunters, rally,
Rally, and ride!

Drink of the magical potion music has mixed
with her wine,
Full of the madness of motion, joyful,
exultant, divine!
Leave all your troubles behind you,
Ride where they never can find you,
Into the gladness of morn,
With the long, clear note of the hunting-horn,
Swiftly o'er hillock and hollow,
Sweeping along with the wind,—
Follow, you hunters, follow,
Follow, and find!

True Pleasures

What will you reach with your riding? What
is the charm of the chase?
Just the delight and the striding swing of the
jubilant pace.
Danger is sweet when you front her,—
In at the death, every hunter!
Now on the breeze the mort is borne
In the long, clear note of the hunting-horn,
Winding merrily, over and over,—
Come, come, come!
Home again, Ranger! home again, Rover!
Turn again, home!

—HENRY VAN DYKE.

Our little lives are kept in equipoise
By opposite attractions and desires;
The struggle of the instinct that enjoys,
And the more noble instinct that aspires.

—LONGFELLOW.

God made all pleasures innocent.

—MRS. NORTON.

True Pleasures

One by one (bright gifts from Heaven)
Joys are sent thee here below;
Take them readily when given,
Ready too, to let them go.
— INGELOW.

The streams of small pleasures fill the lake of happiness.
— SELECTED.

All common things, each day's events,
That with the hour begin and end,
Our pleasures and our discontents,
Are rounds by which we may ascend.
— LONGFELLOW.

There are as many pleasant things,
As many pleasant tones
For those who dwell by cottage hearths,
As those who sit on thrones.
— PHŒBE CARY.

Pleasure and action make the hours seem short.
— SHAKESPEARE.

True Pleasures

A man should endeavour * * * to make the sphere of his innocent pleasures as wide as possible, that he may retire into them with safety, and find in them such a satisfaction as a wise man would not blush to take.

— Addison.

Live while you live, the epicure would say,
And seize the pleasures of the present day;
Live while you live, the sacred preacher cries,
And give to God each moment as it flies;
Lord, in my views let both united be;
I live in pleasure, when I live to thee.

— Doddridge.

Know, dear little one, that Heaven
Does no earthly thing disdain,
Man's poor joys find there an echo
Just as surely as his pain.

— Proctor.

Love's Magic Drops

Love and Light

There are many kinds of love, as many kinds of
light,
And every kind of love makes a glory in the
night.
There is love that stirs the heart, and love that gives it
rest,
But the love that leads life upward is the noblest and
the best.

—Van Dyke.

Be strong to love, O Heart!
Love knows not wrong;
Didst thou love—creatures even,
Life were not long;
Didst thou love God in heaven,
Thou wouldst be strong!

—Proctor.

Love 's a pleasure, solid, real,
Nothing fanciful, ideal,
'T is the bliss of humankind.

—Thomas Chatterton.

Love's Magic Drops

The Prison and the Angel

Self is the only prison that can ever bind the soul;
Love is the only angel who can bid the gates unroll;
And when he comes to call thee, arise and follow fast;
His way may lie through darkness, but it leads to
light at last.

—Van Dyke.

What is love? 'Tis Nature's treasure,
'Tis the storehouse of her joys;
'Tis the highest heaven of pleasure,
'Tis a bliss which never cloys.

—Thomas Chatterton.

There is no service like his that serves because he loves.

—Sir Phillip Sidney.

Life is less than nothing without love.

—Bailey.

Love's Magic Drops

Talk not of wasted affection, affection never was wasted;
If it enrich not the heart of another, its waters, returning
Back to their springs, like the rain, shall fill them full
of refreshment;
That which the fountain sends forth returns again to the
fountain.

—LONGFELLOW.

O merchant at heaven's mart for heavenly ware!
Love is the only coin that passes there.

— FRENCH.

Learn that to love is the one way to know,
Or God or man: it is not love received
That maketh man to know the inner life
Of them that love him; his own love bestowed
Shall do it.

—JEAN INGELOW.

Love is rest.

—BAYARD TAYLOR.

Love's Magic Drops

ONE WORLD

"The worlds in which we live are two,
The world 'I am' and the world 'I do.'"
The worlds in which we live at heart are one,
The world "I am," the fruit of "I have done";
And underneath these worlds of flower and fruit,
The world "I love,"—the only living root.

—VAN DYKE.

The night has a thousand eyes,
And the day but one;
Yet the light of the bright world dies
With the dying sun.

The mind has a thousand eyes,
And the heart but one;
Yet the light of a whole life dies
When love is done.

—FRANCIS WILLIAM BOURDILLON.

Love better is than Fame.

—BAYARD TAYLOR.

Love's Magic Drops

Abou Ben Adhem and the Angel

Abou Ben Adhem (may his tribe increase!)
Awoke one night from a deep dream of peace,
And saw, within the moonlight of his room,
Making it rich, and like a lily in bloom,
An angel writing in a book of gold—
Exceeding peace had made Ben Adhem bold,
And to the presence in the room he said,
"What writest thou?" The vision raised its head,
And with a look made all of sweet accord,
Answer'd, "The names of those who love the Lord."
"And is mine one"? said Abou. "Nay, not so,"
Replied the angel. Abou spoke more low,
But cheerily still, and said, "I pray thee, then,
Write me as one who loves his fellow men."
The angel wrote and vanish'd. The next night
It came again with a great wakening light,
And show'd the names whom love of God had bless'd,
And lo! Ben Adhem's name led all the rest.

—Leigh Hunt.

Whoever lives true life will love true love.

—Mrs. Browning.

Love's Magic Drops

Love, indeed, is light from heaven;
A spark of that immortal fire
With angels shared, by Allah given,
To lift from earth our low desire.
Devotion wafts the mind above,
But heaven itself descends in love;
A feeling from the Godhead caught,
To wean from self each sordid thought;
A ray of Him who form'd the whole;
A glory circling round the soul!

— Byron.

Love is too precious to be named,
Save with a reverence deep and high.

— Alice Cary.

I hold it true, whate'er befall,
I feel it when I sorrow most;
'T is better to have loved and lost,
Than never to have loved at all.

— Tennyson.

Love comforteth, like sunshine after rain.

— Shakespeare.

Love's Magic Drops

True love's the gift which God has given
To man alone beneath the heaven;
It is not fantasy's hot fire,
Whose wishes, soon as granted, fly;
It liveth not in fierce desire,
With dead desire it doth not die;
It is the secret sympathy,
The silver link, the silken tie,
Which heart to heart, and mind to mind,
In body and in soul can bind.

— Scott.

He asked her once again, "What hearest thou?
What means the voice of Life?" She answered, "Love!
For love is life and they who do not love
Are not alive. But every soul that loves,
Lives in the heart of God and hears Him speak."

— Van Dyke.

Love rules the court, the camp, the grove,
And men below, and saints above;
For love is heaven, and heaven is love.

— Sir Walter Scott.

Merriment

A LITTLE of thy merriment,
Of thy sparkling, light content,
Give me, my cheerful brook,—
That I may still be full of glee
And gladsomeness, where'er I be,
Though fickle fate hath prisoned me
In some neglected nook.

— LOWELL.

Cheeriness is a thing to be more profoundly grateful for than all that genius ever inspired or talent ever accomplished. Next best to natural, spontaneous cheeriness is deliberate, intended and persistent cheeriness, which we can create, can cultivate, and can so foster and cherish that after a few years the world will never suspect it was not a hereditary gift.

— HELEN HUNT JACKSON.

A laugh is worth a hundred groans in any market.

— ROSSETTI.

Laugh if you are wise.

— ADDISON.

Merriment

Bear through sorrow, wrong, and ruth,
In thy heart the dew of youth,
On thy lips the smile of truth.

Oh, that dew, like balm, shall steal
Into wounds that cannot heal,
Even as sleep our eyes doth seal;

And that smile, like sunshine, dart
Into many a sunless heart,
For a smile of God thou art.

— LONGFELLOW.

'T is not in title nor in rank,
'T is not in wealth like London bank,
To make us truly blest.
If happiness have not her seat
And center in the breast,
We may be wise, or rich or great,
But never can be blest.

— SELECTED.

Smiles live long after frowns have faded.

— JAMES A. GARFIELD.

Merriment

SEASONS

'T is April in November,
If you will make it so,
Or Maytime in December,
Despite the falling snow,
If only you'll remember
Your smiles make roses blow.

'T is spring in autumn weather
If you will sing all day,
And smiles and songs together
Turn winter into May;
The snow will be like heather
If only *you* are gay.

—SELECTED.

Joy is the mainspring in the whole
Of endless Nature's calm rotation.
Joy moves the dazzling wheels that roll
In the great Timepiece of Creation.

—SCHILLER.

A good laugh is sunshine in the house.

—THACKERAY.

Merriment

Joy and Duty

"Joy is a Duty,"—so with golden lore
The Hebrew rabbis taught in days of yore,
And happy human hearts heard in their speech
Almost the highest wisdom man can reach.

But one bright peak still rises far above,
And there the Master stands, whose name is Love,
Saying to those whom weary tasks employ:
"Life is divine when Duty is a Joy."

—Van Dyke.

The merriest folks are the best, I know,
For those who are laughing and gay,
Are the ones who are willing to stop and show
Tired people an easier way.

—Caro A. Dugan.

The sunshine of life is made up of very little beams, which are bright all the time.

—Selected.

Merriment

Hence we may learn,
That though it be a grand and comely thing
To be unhappy,—(and we think it is,
Because so many grand and clever folk
Have found out reasons for unhappiness)
* * * yet, since we are not grand,
O, not at all, and as for cleverness,
That may or may not be,—it is well
For us to be as happy as we can!

—JEAN INGELOW.

The world is so full of a number of things,
I'm sure we should all be as happy as kings.

—R. L. STEVENSON.

All who joy would win
Must share it,—happiness was born a twin.

—BYRON.

It's gude to be merry and wise.

—OLD SCOTCH SONG.

Merriment

I opened the doors of my heart. And behold,
There was music within and a song,
And echoes did feed on the sweetness, repeating it long.
I opened the doors of my heart. And behold,
There was music that played itself out in æolian notes;
Then was heard, as a far-away bell at long intervals tolled.

—Jean Ingelow.

What then remains, but well our power to use,
And keep good humor still, whate'er we lose?
And trust me, dear, good humor can prevail,
When airs, and flights, and screams, and scolding, fail.

— Pope.

It is good
To lengthen to the last a sunny mood.

— Lowell.

A merry heart goes all the day.

— Shakespeare.

Orisons

Faith

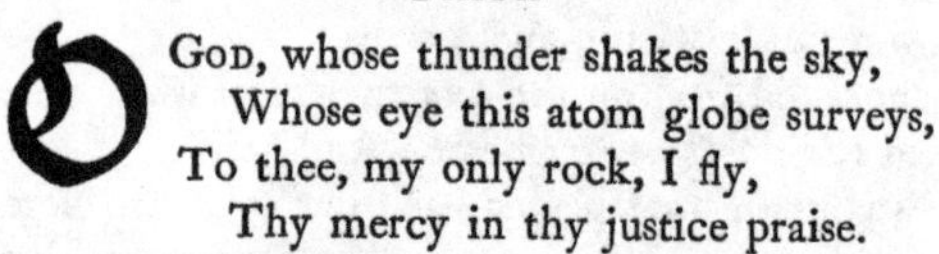

O God, whose thunder shakes the sky,
Whose eye this atom globe surveys,
To thee, my only rock, I fly,
Thy mercy in thy justice praise.

The mystic mazes of thy will,
The shadows of celestial light,
Are past the power of human skill;
But what the Eternal acts is right.

O, teach me in the trying hour,
When anguish swells the dewy tear,
To still my sorrows, own thy power,
Thy goodness love, thy justice fear.

— Thomas Chatterton.

A good man's prayers
Will from the deepest dungeon climb Heaven's height
And bring a blessing down.

— Joanna Baillie.

Prayer is the spirit speaking truth to Truth.

— Bailey.

"Yet all this may not bring happiness
Except in your Orisons you lift your voice
To Him who holds the gift of health"

Orisons

For All These

I thank thee, Lord, that I am straight and strong,
With wit to work and hope to keep me brave;
That two-score years, unfathomed, still belong
To the allotted life thy bounty gave.

I thank thee that the sight of sunlit lands
And dipping hills, the breath of evening grass—
That wet, dark rocks and flowers in my hands
Can give me daily gladness as I pass.

I thank thee that I love the things of earth—
Ripe fruits and laughter lying down to sleep,
The shine of lighted towns, the graver worth
Of beating human hearts that laugh and weep.

I thank thee that as yet I need not know,
Yet need not fear, the mystery of the end;
But more than all, and though all these should go—
Dear Lord, this on my knees!—I thank thee
for my friend.

—Juliet Wilbor Tompkins.

A prayer, in its simplest definition, is merely a wish turned Godward.

—Phillips Brooks.

Orisons

The prayer of Ajax was for light;
Through all that dark and desperate fight,
The blackness of that noonday night,
He asked but the return of sight,
To see his foeman's face.

Let our unceasing, earnest prayer
Be, too, for light,—for strength to bear
Our portion of the weight of care
That crushes into dumb despair
One-half the human race.

—Longfellow.

More things are wrought by prayer
Than this world dreams of.

—Tennyson.

Be not afraid to pray—to pray is right.
Pray, if thou canst, with hope; but ever pray,
Though hope be weak or sick with long delay;
Pray in the darkness if there be no light.

—Hartley Coleridge.

Orisons

MATINS

Flowers, when the night is done,
Lift their heads to greet the sun;
Sweetest looks and odours raise,
In a silent hymn of praise.

So my heart would turn away
From the darkness to the day;
Lying open, in God's sight,
As a flower in the light.

— VAN DYKE.

Not what we wish, but what we want,
Oh! let thy grace supply,
The good unask'd, in mercy grant;
The ill, though ask'd, deny.

— MERRICK.

---

* * * O Lord, to me impart
An innocent and grateful heart,
That after my last sleep I may
Awake to thy eternal day! Amen.

— S. T. COLERIDGE.

COSIMO is an innovative publisher of books that inspire, inform, and engage readers worldwide.

COSIMO was inspired by Cosimo de Medici, the first of the de Medici dynasty, who ignited the most important cultural and artistic revolution in Western history — the Renaissance.

Cosimo de Medici, the quintessential Renaissance man, was a banker, political leader, scholar, and patron of the arts. He had a passion for the pursuit of knowledge, and he breathed new life into the study of the ancient past. He enriched Florence by building palaces and churches and by sponsoring libraries, where professional scribes copied classics from antiquity into the finest manuscripts.

This quest for enrichment is the foundation for **COSIMO,** an innovative publisher of books that inspire, inform, and engage readers worldwide. **COSIMO CLASSICS** brings to life unique, out-of-print classics, representing subjects as diverse as *Alternative Health, Business and Economics, Eastern Philosophy, Personal Growth, Mythology, Philosophy, Sacred Texts, Science, Spirituality,* and much more!

COSIMO CLASSICS uses state-of-the art technology to publish distinctive, high-quality books that are always available online at affordable prices.

COSIMO CLASSICS uses state-of-the-art technology to publish distinctive, high-quality books. In our pursuit for enrichment, our commitment to you is that **COSIMO CLASSICS** offers:

- **Permanent Availability:** Our books never go out of print.

- **Global Availability**: Our books are available online at www.cosimobooks.com, www.amazon.com, www.barnesandnoble.com, and other online bookstores, and can be ordered from your favorite local bookstore, too.

- **Special Quantity Discounts:** Our books are available at special quantity discounts for bulk purchases, sales promotions, premiums, or fund raising. For more information, please contact us at info@cosimobooks.com.

- **Free e-Newsletter:** Sign up for our e-newsletter at www.cosimobooks.com to discover what's happening at **COSIMO** and to receive announcements of our new books, free excerpts, and special offers.

Your Favorite Out-of-Print Books: If you know of any books that you would like to see republished as a **COSIMO CLASSIC**, drop us a line at info@cosimobooks.com.

A complete collection of **COSIMO CLASSICS** is always available at our website, www.cosimobooks.com.

Printed in the USA
CPSIA information can be obtained
at www.ICGtesting.com
LVHW041208220424
778085LV00001B/149